IMAGES
of England

AROUND
SNODLAND

IMAGES
of England

AROUND
SNODLAND

Andrew Ashbee

TEMPUS

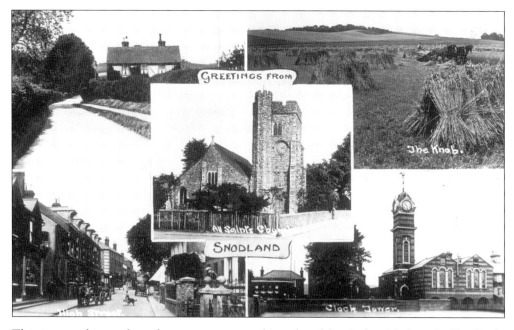

This is one of a number of composite postcards produced by Arthur Nethersole Hambook, Snodland's most avid photographer for nearly fifty years. We would be immeasurably the poorer without his fine series of views of Snodland and district. These began to be published around 1904 and continued until the early 1950s. He sometimes reissued pictures many years after their first appearance. Sadly all his plates were destroyed after his death. This postcard was still in circulation in the early 1930s, but some individual views from it might first have appeared ten years or so earlier.

Frontispiece: The ferry at Snodland was at its busiest when the cement factories were working on both sides of the river. Up to 600 persons a day were noted as crossing in the 1880s.

First published 2003

Tempus Publishing Limited
The Mill, Brimscombe Port,
Stroud, Gloucestershire, GL5 2QG

British Library Cataloguing in Publication Data.
A catalogue record for this book is available from the British Library.

ISBN 0 7524 2823 3

Typesetting and origination by Tempus Publishing Limited
Printed in Great Britain by Midway Colour Print, Wiltshire

Contents

Acknowledgements

Originals or copies of all the pictures are in the collection of Snodland Historical Society at Snodland Millennium Museum. Special thanks are due to John Soane and to Edward S. Gowers for the loan of many items from their splendid collections, and also to D. Anstey, Mrs Butcher, Mrs J. Capon, D. Fielder, C. Greene, J. Hamilton, J. Hammond, Holmesdale Technology College, R. Hunt, Mrs D. Jell, Mrs J. Joyce, the Kent Messenger Group, O. Lambert, Mrs M. Lawrence, M. Ocock, Mrs M. Penney, R. Penny, B. Pentecost, St Katherine's School, Snodland CE Primary School, Mrs M. Stockford, and the Women's Institute of Ham Hill and Snodland for the use of other pictures included here.

This has been a favourite view of Snodland photographers over many years. The probable date of this picture is around 1910.

Introduction

The legacy of row upon row of utilitarian houses of the last 130 years or so in both Snodland and Halling obscures the long history attached to both parishes. The local landscape too has suffered much from chalk extraction and from industrial development. Yet it should be remembered that the latter has brought prosperity and growth to both communities. The pretty village of Birling gives an inkling of what Snodland and Halling would have looked like 150 years ago, when agricultural life and labour still held sway. Indeed in 1821 Birling boasted eighty-two houses to Snodland's meagre fifty-nine.

For early man the banks of the Medway in these parts offered all that was required: water, pasture, arable and wood land were all readily available, settlement could be sited above the flood plain and the river itself provided a means of communication. The river was also a barrier to be crossed, and here too, convenient ways were found. 'Halling Man', dated to around 2000 BC, was discovered in 1912, and later a boat was found which he may have used. In Snodland a ring-ditch of the late Bronze Age had been sited at the highest point of the chalk outcrop known locally as 'The Knob'. In time the Romans settled the valley, leaving their mark in villas and burial tumuli. Both are found in Snodland. It has been suggested that the first Roman advance to conquer Britain in AD 43 may have crossed the Medway at Snodland or nearby. Then the Saxons came, evidently settling at Holborough for a time and burying their dead on the hill above, between the prehistoric ring-ditch and a Roman tumulus.

By fair means or foul the monks of Rochester obtained title to Snodland, and by the time the Domesday survey was made Snodland and Halling were part of the holdings of the Bishop of Rochester. At the end of the eleventh century Bishop Gundulph built a palace at Halling which was used by his successors until the 1500s. Part of a single wall remains. The Bishop's bailiff controlled the estates: records for the manor of Halling (with Snodland and Cuxton) are not extant before 1702, by which time the twice-yearly meetings of tenants were held at the Five Bells public house in Halling High Street. The Bishop's mill was at Holborough. Following the Battle of Hastings Birling was given to Odo, Bishop of Bayeux (as indeed was Halling at that time), but the main residents resided at Birling Place. From 1435 these were the Nevills, Earls of Abergavenny, whose descendants are still there. Neither Snodland nor Halling had such distinguished inhabitants, but the Bishop's Palace at Halling was at one time home to the famous lawyer and historian William Lambarde, and subsequently to the Dalison family. The Marshams, Earls of Romney, acquired Whorne's Place on the Halling-Cuxton border and in time they purchased large parts of local parishes, including Snodland and Halling. In Snodland the principal house was Holloway Court at Holborough. This was home to the wealthiest parishioners, including John May, whose father had built a new paper mill at Snodland around

1740. Whether or not there was a previous paper mill on the site we cannot say from the evidence available, but this one continues to the present day. From small beginnings it grew a little after 1800, importing owners and workers from paper-making regions elsewhere, but the real development came after 1854 when the mill was acquired by the Hook family. New manufacturing techniques and the coming of the railway in 1856, added to Charles Townsend Hook's energy, led to an increase in production from five to seventy tons weekly in little over twenty years. Today the mill runs two production lines: packaging paper made from waste and a high quality white-coated paper from imported wood pulp.

The other principal industry has been lime and cement manufacture. Small-scale lime working had existed in the district for centuries, but during the nineteenth century several firms were established and production increased. Lime for building the Waterloo and New London bridges came from Halling. The first factory in the area was created at North Halling at Whorne's Place in 1799. By 1817 Poynder and Medlicott had begun quarrying on the Snodland-Halling boundary and this enterprise was taken over by William Lee in 1846. In the 1850s Charles Formby began a new lime works at Halling, later reconstituted by Albert Batchelor, and in the 1870s Hilton and Anderson inaugurated their Halling Manor Lime and Cement Works. On the opposite side of the river the Peters brothers established what was said to be the largest cement works in the world. The last of the works was built by W.L.H. Roberts in 1923 at Holborough. Most of these firms were swept into the Association of Portland Cement Manufacturers and ceased operations before the Second World War, although the Holborough works is set to be revived and there is still a major works at Halling.

The enormous labour forces once required to dig chalk or make paper have been largely replaced by machines and advances in technology, and today, with the M2 and M20 a few minutes drive away, and the railway, the parishioners of Snodland, Halling and Birling are just as likely to work elsewhere as in their own community. Housing continues to increase as derelict chalk pits are eyed as ideal 'brown field' sites by builders, while the proximity of motorways has also attracted a new industry in the form of vast retail distribution warehouses.

One

Remnants
of Ancient Times

Alexander Thomson (the man second from left) supervising the harvesting of the land belonging to his Covey Hall Farm. Behind is the hill known locally as 'The Knob', which was clearly of great significance to early inhabitants. Before it was completely removed by chalk quarrying, a Bronze Age ring-ditch surrounding a burial site was discovered at the summit. To the north of this was a Saxon cemetery, in which thirty-nine graves were recorded – some others had probably already been lost. On the extreme right the clump of trees marks the site of a Roman tumulus. Apart from the main cremation burial, a secondary one was later added of a child, aged about one, in a fine lead coffin (which is now in Maidstone Museum).

It is possible that the river crossing at Snodland was used by the invading Romans in AD 43. Certainly they settled in the area and a substantial Roman villa was built at Snodland. Several excavations of it have been made, but as this bleak picture of work in 1964 shows, archaeologists have been handicapped by later industrial use of the site. The square feature on the right-hand side of the picture is a cold plunge-bath, or possibly a storage tank.

Visitors at an open day listen to Albert Daniels explaining excavations at the Snodland Roman Villa, October 1985.

Another view at the same open day, with the late Arthur Harrison expounding on the 'channelled hypocaust' seen in the picture.

A hard base across the river – whether man-made or natural is not known – allowed passage from earliest times. This picture at low tide shows the shallows called 'Snodland Rocks'.

The ancient river crossing surely contributed to Snodland's origins. The Snodland Ferry was plying its trade by the 1840s, but is probably not as old as the Halling-Wouldham Ferry a mile or so to the north. This picture shows it in 1904.

The author's grandparents and their friends are here about to embark for the Burham side in 1924. Returning passengers would strike an old tin kettle at the hut to call the ferryman to fetch them. The ferry closed in 1948.

The 'K' on the tug identifies it as belonging to Knight's, long established in the Medway towns. At one time the owner lived in The Cedars in Snodland. All the ferry apparatus and buildings – except for the ferry house – have now disappeared.

From earliest times the river has been heavily used for commercial enterprise. The red-sail barges of the Thames and Medway were a familiar sight for generations. Paper and cement were the principal commodities in these parts. Here a tug with its barges has just navigated the horseshoe bend and is passing the Snodland Ferry.

13

A tranquil scene on the Brook (the common pasture belonging to the parish) around the end of the nineteenth century.

The bridge leading to Willow Walk on the Brook, 1938. Selected trees from here were felled from time to time for the manufacture of cricket bats.

Two
Heading East

'Veles' was for many years the home of the Hook family, owners of the Snodland paper mill. Something of what Snodland owes to the benefactions of this family will become clear in the course of this book. Pictured here in 1929, the house was demolished the following year after the death of the last of the family, Maude Midsummer Hook. Today the bypass runs in a cutting across this spot.

This seems to be the earliest photograph yet known of the top of the High Street. The shoe shop (second on the left) had been taken over by Charles Betts by 1899, although here it still carries Bolger's name.

Probably slightly later (and postmarked 1907), this picture postcard shows the post office where William Bateman was postmaster between about 1894 and 1909.

A view down the High Street from around 1910, with the Congregational church to the left and the entrance to the rectory on the right.

In the later nineteenth century some large houses were built opposite the Rectory Meadow (part of the original glebe land). From right to left they were an unnamed villa, Auburn (a surgery), Homeleigh (the manse for the New Jerusalem church) and Trefoy.

Anchor Place was built in the 1860s for the village coal merchant, Thomas William Peters. He also built Hope Terrace next door, intending it for family members, but only one – his son Nathan – ever took up the offer.

William Gorham (1759-1820) inherited land in 1803 and seems to have built these houses soon after (with one 'converted from a stable' in 1838). They were always called Gorham's Cottages, but since they jutted into the High Street they were demolished in the 1970s when increased traffic caused concern.

The front entrance of Ivymeath, home of Colonel James Trevenan Holland, manager of the paper mill following the death of Charles Townsend Hook in 1877. It had been built by 1881, but within a few years the Colonel had moved to Tunbridge Wells. This photograph, together with the one below, dates from 1906.

Ivymeath from the south west. The building was enlarged when it became the headquarters of the Mid-Kent Water Company.

The Hook family took pride in providing amenities for Snodland. The public baths in Queen's Avenue were a gift by Agnes and Maude Hook to the parish in 1900. They remained in use until 1974, by which time most houses had their own bathrooms. The building is now a private house. This illustration comes from the illuminated address of thanks from the parish council to the Hook sisters.

Although the Devonshire Rooms, opened in 1895, primarily served the Sunday school of the New Jerusalem church, from the first they have also been used by societies and for Snodland's public meetings. The town council offices are now housed there too.

Agnes and Maude Hook gave these almshouses in Waghorn Road in memory of their brother Eustace (died 1890). They were opened on 27 December 1893.

The Hook sisters gave a second set of almshouses in 1903 in memory of their governess, Amelia Drummond. Unfortunately Agnes Hook died shortly before they were completed. Today it is required of tenants of all the almshouses that they are aged sixty or more, and have been resident in Snodland for at least ten years.

This view seems to date from around 1930. The Red Lion public house is one of Snodland's few remaining ancient buildings. In medieval times the market cross stood outside. Here the Westminster Bank is next door, while the grocer's shop opposite had served the community since the mid-nineteenth century.

A mulberry tree in the garden gave Mulberry Cottage its familiar name. Originally a mid-fifteenth-century hall house, it was extensively restored in 1932.

Most traces of Brook Street have gone. Sweetbriar Cottage was demolished around 1930 as part of the development of the 'Veles' site and its garden.

As this picture shows, Alma Place, leading west from Brook Street, was little more than a footpath. Locals always referred to it as 'Cat's Alley' after a Mr Cat or Catt. The gardener's cottage to Ivymeath peeps over the wall on the right, with Ivymeath itself facing the viewer. Shortly after this picture was taken the houses were demolished to make way for the bypass.

The railway from Strood to Maidstone opened in 1856 and contributed greatly to Snodland's development. This picture of the lower end of the High Street dates from around 1910.

A view of the High Street from the opposite direction, taken at around the same time as the previous picture. On the extreme left is Nyanza House (now May Place), built as the village surgery in 1868 when Charles White, the first doctor, arrived. On the right is the Queen's Hotel, built in 1856 to accompany the opening of the railway. This was also a popular venue for parish meetings.

Three
Heading North

Originally called North Street, Holborough Road leads to Holborough, Halling and the Medway towns. The presence of the cinema shows that this picture dates from 1912 or after. In the distance the road was widened in 1927. No doubt the children are heading home from the British Schools.

The cinema in Holborough Road was opened on 23 March 1912. When the rival Wardona opened in 1938 on the High Street, it was forced to close and the building eventually became the Catholic church.

No doubt many of the children above attended the British Schools further along Holborough Road. This was built in 1857 to cater for those unwilling to receive the Church of England dogma promoted by the National Schools. The clock tower was erected in 1878 as a memorial to Charles Townsend Hook. It survives today, although the school buildings have gone.

Covey Hall farmhouse was rebuilt to its present state in 1881, although the farm was of great antiquity. Before the growth of the village its land stretched on either side of the main road, but building and chalk extraction encroached to such an extent that it became unviable as a farm by the mid-twentieth century.

Prospect Cottage began as a fifteenth-century hall house – to which the brick portion was added in around 1780 by Jasper Crothall, owner of the paper mill. The southern end served as a butcher's shop from around 1785 to the mid-twentieth century.

In 1874 William Lee, owner of the cement works, built the Institute as a working men's club. For many years it also served the whole community as a place for entertainments and meetings and, for a time, the library was housed there. Eventually the club moved to new premises opposite, converted from the Snodland branch of the Rochester and District Co-operative Society, and the old building was demolished.

Here is the Co-operative Society building in the year of its opening, 1912. Having made several moves, the business took over and enlarged the post office building in December 2001. The two companies now share the premises

Holborough Road, looking north. A bus is waiting at the usual stop.

This picture appears to show an outing from the working men's club (situated behind the farm building on the left), in 1924.

Approaching Holborough along Holborough Road, with the Prince of Wales public house on the left and part of Victoria or 'Lee's' cottages on the right. Nothing in this picture (which probably dates from the 1930s) remains today.

The Rising Sun was made from two old houses in the mid-nineteenth century. Here it is shortly before closure and demolition in 1984 to make way for the bypass. Its situation beside the cement works was good for trade!

A mill at Holborough is mentioned in the first Snodland charter, dated AD 838 (although the document is believed to be a tenth-century forgery!) It was rebuilt to its present form in 1881 by William Lee, but ceased working quite early in the twentieth century.

To the south of the mill is Island Cottage, seen here from the rear, with Mill Stream Cottage on the opposite side of what was, until 1850, the road to Halling.

Holborough Court was built in 1886 for William Henry Roberts, owner of the local cement works. It replaced Holloway Court, which had been sited near the water mill, using some materials from the old house. Roberts had an active social life and was friends with Edward, Prince of Wales (later Edward VII). His son, William Lee Henry Roberts, was a bachelor who preferred to live in Mill Stream Cottage. Holborough Court was demolished in 1932, soon after the estate was acquired from the family by Associated Portland Cement Manufacturers. Extensive grounds included a polo field, which was sometimes also used for Snodland fêtes and sports. Front (above) and rear views are shown.

These two pictures of the exterior and interior of Mill Stream Cottage (also called Little Holborough) formed part of William Lee Henry Roberts' Christmas card for 1923.

This old house, on the old road from Holborough to Halling, still stands but is now isolated. It was once home to several managers of the cement works from the early nineteenth century onwards.

The Cedars seems to have been a replacement for Gilder's Farm, which was in the path of the railway, opened in 1856. The old road passed across the foreground.

Four

Heading West

The Lodge in the upper High Street was built around 1841 for Thomas Fletcher Waghorn (1800-1850) who established the Overland Route to India via Egypt in the mid-1830s. He was a man of great energy and enterprise, but a combination of bad luck and government indifference to his scheme led to mounting debts, and he died a broken man. He is buried in All Saints churchyard.

The name 'Wardona' for the cinema – the result of a £10 prize offered by the *Kent Messenger* – came from 'Harry Ward, owner', and was suggested by Mrs Dungate of Snodland. Later called the Savoy, it closed in 1963, thereafter becoming a bingo club and snooker hall.

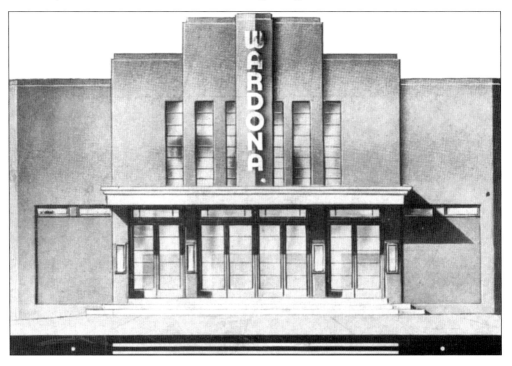

This picture comes from the first Wardona programme, issued on 21 March 1938.

A trip to the hop fields leaves The Bull in 1908.

In the early nineteenth century Dodnor Cottages were converted into houses for farm workers from a single large medieval house called Benet's Place.

Gammon's upper shop situated on the corner of Birling Road and Paddlesworth Road. Mr Frederick Gammon stands in the doorway to his bakery. Stables for the firm's horses were on the opposite side of the road.

The approach to Woodlands or 'Cox's' Farm. The nineteenth-century wing which is visible here was built by Joseph Champion in 1881 when he took over the farm.

Cox's Cottages date from around the seventeenth century and were occupied by farm labourers.

Mark Farm before its recent renovation. It takes its name from its position on the Snodland-Paddlesworth boundary and can be traced back to around 1300.

Until 1888 Paddlesworth was a parish in its own right. This picture from around 1908 shows that a series of gates across the road helped control the livestock.

In spite of the fences one sheep seems to have escaped to munch the greener grass on the other side!

Although Henry VIII purloined the revenues and disposed of the Rectorship, the little Norman church at Paddlesworth survived as a farm outbuilding. It continued in this way until the 1930s when the Roberts family decided to restore it as a private chapel.

The renovated building in 1935. In 1951 Paddlesworth church was purchased by the Bishop of Rochester and later devolved to the Churches Conservation Trust, which now looks after it.

The parish of Dode was joined to Paddlesworth in 1366, following decimation of the population by the Black Death. The church fell into ruin, as the above picture of 1896 shows.

In 1906 Dode church was purchased by George Arnold, Mayor of Gravesend, and restored as an example of rural Norman architecture. This picture was taken at its completion. The church is now in private hands and occasional services are held there.

The farm at Great Buckland, before it was totally destroyed in a fire in 1911. Dode church is nearby and the former parish of Dode included part of the Manor of Buckland.

Hop-picking at Great Buckland around 1900. Once hop-growing flourished throughout the area, but it declined substantially during the nineteenth century.

The ancient track called 'The Pilgrim's Way' runs along the foot of the Downs above Snodland.

This beautiful area is known as 'Happy Valley' to local people.

44

Five
Heading South

In early days travellers on their way south from Snodland journeyed via Birling Road and Hollow Lane, but in 1825/26 a turnpike road was authorized from Strood to Malling, with toll-gates at Strood, Snodland and Leybourne. The Snodland gate was at the crossroads, and Malling Road was part of the new turnpike running straight to Ham Hill. Tolls ceased in 1878. There were no houses built until the 1870s – and then only the first twenty on each side. Here is the road in 1904.

The main crossroads in the 1920s. Gammon's bakery had taken over from John Horton in 1910 and Dennant's electrical shop had replaced Daniel Chalklen's cycle shop, although Chalklen's advertisement can still be seen.

This view from the opposite direction probably dates from the 1930s. The row of shops from Collison the butcher to Dedrick the grocer are all making use of their awnings on a sunny day.

Another view of the lower end of Malling Road, probably from the 1920s, and again without a car in sight!

The forge and garage of Charles (and later Frederick) Hinds was built in 1903. This picture can be dated between 20 December 1914 and Easter Monday 1915, when the 15th Middlesex Regiment was billeted in Snodland. Horses have given way to cars and today Snodland Central Garage occupies the site.

This view north from the corner of Bramley Road appears to date from soon after 1900.

A view of Bramley Road in 1911 from the west, looking towards Malling Road.

Christian Pries outside his general stores opposite Oxford Street. He was in business here by 1907 and the shop was run by the family until September 1971.

The new path is the clue that this picture dates from 1910.

The upper end of Malling Road in the 1930s. Plots of land were sold for housing in 1892 and pairs of semi-detached houses were built on most plots.

Woodbank House, next to Christ Church, was the most imposing of the houses on the east side.

St Katherine's House was built in the 1890s for Archibald Woodburn, who was secretary of the paper mill between 1891 and 1906. When this photograph was taken in 1917 it was occupied by a Belgian family who had fled their war-torn country.

This sixteenth-century cottage was in Bedlam Lane (now St Katherine's Lane) opposite Christ Church. It is possible that its once isolated position made it an ideal residence for afflicted persons, but by the early 1700s it had become a family home. It was demolished in 1974.

Residents of School Lane, Ham Hill, in around 1930.

Ham Hill School catered for up to seventy pupils in its time. This infant class from 1930 are, from left to right: ? Fuller, I. Revill, ? Burr, B. Dean, A. Skinner, S. Harper, E. Dean, T. Joy, H. Jenkins, K. Mitchell, R. Cogger, E. Austin, M. Chapman, W. Lamb, R. Cogger, ? Fuller, B. Fuller, ? Banfield, J. Perkin, S. Mason, ? Banfield.

The Freemasons Arms, Ham Hill, and the entrance to Brook Lane, 1947. The name 'Freemasons Arms' seems to have replaced 'The Bell' quite early in the nineteenth century.

Dykes Cottages were on the south side of Brook Lane.

A rare survivor of old Ham Hill is Ham Mill Cottage in Brook Lane. It is believed that a paper mill operated here, or close by, and that some of the timbers in this building came from Chatham dockyard.

Six
Churches

A familiar view of the parish church of All Saints at the east end of Snodland's High Street.

An exterior view of All Saints in 1904. The organ chamber was enlarged to make the present vestry in 1909. Most of the gravestones were moved to the north wall of the churchyard in the 1950s to enable easier maintainence of the grounds.

This interior view of All Saints church dates from 1898. The east window depicting four Protestant martyrs (destroyed by bombing in 1942) was put in by Henry Dampier Phelps, Rector between 1804 and 1865. The chancel floor was lower then.

A remarkable feature within All Saints is this incised picture of the Crucifixion, an object of great veneration to fourteenth and fifteenth-century parishioners. Evidently it was covered over at the Reformation and was rediscovered in 1870 during restoration work. The Victorians delighted in colouring it again.

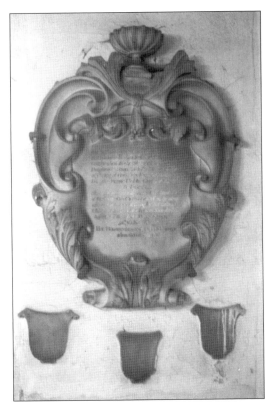

On the north wall of the nave is this memorial to Martha Manley, wife of Sir Richard Manley of Holloway Court, Holborough. She died on 29 March 1682, aged fifty-eight. Her husband died on 29 April 1684. His tomb beneath the nave floor was briefly revealed during repairs in 2002. Expert opinion is that Martha's memorial is the work of Artus Quellin III, partner to the more famous Grinling Gibbons. Gibbons left much of his commissions in stone to Quellin while he himself worked in wood.

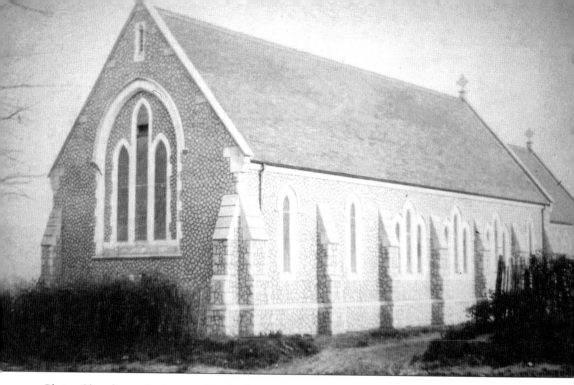

Christ Church was built as a chapel-of-ease to Birling, to serve a fast-growing community at Ham Hill and parishioners south of the old Snodland boundary. Work began on 1 March 1892, and the foundation stone was laid by the Hon. Mrs Ralph Nevill of Birling on 30 April 1893, with the inaugural service held on 10 October 1893. This photograph probably dates from the building's completion.

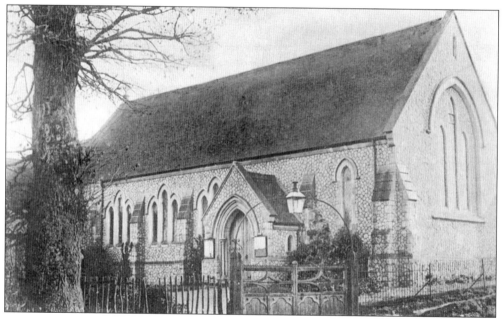

The church was built by the firm of Robert Langridge at Ham Hill to a design by Percy Monckton. This view from the north west dates from 1904. A proposed tower was never built.

In the early nineteenth century two paper mill managers encouraged Nonconformist worship in Snodland. Houses were at first licensed for this and two cottages near the mill later became the first chapel.

In 1854 a new purpose-built chapel was erected in Holborough Road. The first service was held on Good Friday, 6 April 1855. Within three years the British Schools (offering an alternative to the Church of England education favoured in the National Schools) opened on the same site.

After this larger chapel was opened in the High Street in 1888, the British School acquired the old chapel for its infant department. Later it became home to a variety of industrial uses until it was demolished in 1997. Methodists and Congregationalists joined in 1976 to make the present United Church.

The church of St John the Baptist (or the church of the New Jerusalem) was consecrated on 27 June 1882. Worship followed the teachings of Emanuel Swedenborg (1688-1772), a polymath who expounded his spiritual experiences gained through dreams and visions. Anna Maria Hook, wife of the paper mill manager, had adopted Swedenborg's doctrines in Norwich from around 1831, and the family kept their own resident minister on moving to Gloucestershire. Arriving in Snodland in 1856 they at first worshipped in the home of one of their employees (several of whom had been Swedenborgians in Gloucestershire and Wiltshire). On 26 June 1864 they opened a chapel within their family home of 'Veles'. By the late 1870s plans were in hand for a separate church. It cost £5,000 and was paid for by the Hook family and Colonel Holland.

The east end of the New Jerusalem church, *c.* 1950.

An early view of the chancel. Note the fine gas lighting. The lectern was given by the Snodland papermakers in 1892, and is now housed in a church in America.

In 1928 the Salvation Army moved to this building in Malling Road, having previously used a school hut in Oxford Street. They now meet in the Devonshire Rooms and various other venues.

The Baptists in Snodland first worshipped in the Institute in Holborough Road, but in 1898 this iron room with a porch was built for them in Church Field. In 1939 services were transferred to Halling and the building was acquired by the Lead Wool Company for a canteen. It was demolished in 1982.

The foundation stone of the Primitive Methodist chapel in Malling Road was laid on 14 November 1877, services previously having been held in the open air and in a house in Brook Street. The Sunday school building, at the rear, was added in 1899. The whole building was sold in 1976, after the Methodists joined forces with the Congregational Church in the High Street, and is currently a car showroom.

Catholics in Snodland at first worshipped at the Institute, but from wartime onwards they had the use of the Holborough Road cinema building, and later acquired it.

In August 1987, 560 Jehovah's Witnesses came from all over the country to build the Kingdom Hall in Snodland on previously-laid foundations in only three days.

In 1882 W.H. Roberts gave a mission church to Holborough in memory of his father-in-law William Lee, and in 1889 he gave a similar one (pictured here) to Upper Halling. Both have been demolished.

Seven

Events

A group of Volunteers at work on the Downs in 1916, during the First World War. The men at the back, from left to right, are: W. Tapley, S. Gooding, -?- , A. Penny, A. Simms, W.L.H. Roberts, H. Pile, P. Bridger, E. Thorndycraft, F. Hales, A. State, A. Lucas, E.H. Edgeler, W. Pay, W. Hilder, ? May. In front, with his son, is ? Hollands.

Israel May, stationed in Snodland, was the first policeman to be murdered in Kent. His attacker, Thomas Atkins, had been drinking and struck May in a fight on the night of Sunday 24 August 1873. May's body was discovered the next day and Atkins was arrested a few days later. He was convicted of manslaughter rather than murder and ordered to be kept in penal servitude for twenty years. A memorial stone to PC May was erected beside Malling Road, and this was later set in the bank of the adjacent stream. When the stream was piped and Rocfort Road was built, the stone was removed in pieces to the cemetery.

A mourning card issued at the time of PC May's death. A subscription was raised for his widow and children which was generously supported. The funeral was attended by the whole community and by many representatives from police forces throughout the south-east.

This is evidently one of the parades arranged by the Ancient Order of Foresters. The float seems to have a patriotic theme which may link it with the Coronation of Edward VII in 1902.

A church parade of the Ancient Order of Foresters, Snodland branch, with the firemen and Salvation Army band to the fore. The scene is thought to date from 1906. Note the screen on the left where Lee Road was to be built; also the early car.

An accident in which a paraffin lamp ignited a rope caused the great paper mill fire of Sunday 12 August 1906. The mill was totally destroyed and 400 men lost their jobs. Evidence of the immediate local concern is shown by the crowd gathered nearby.

Fortunately there was no loss of life and the event soon took on a sight-seeing attraction. Many postcards were produced and tours of the site took place.

Clearly the ruins became an adventure playground for local boys!

Six fire brigades attended the fire from Snodland, Halling, Malling, Maidstone, Rochester and Chatham, but a shortage of water hampered their efforts.

Two barges were also destroyed in the fire. One is buried beneath the debris shown in this photograph.

Rebuilding took two years, and as much employment as possible in this redevelopment was given to the mill workers themselves. Here is the coal wharf at the north end of the site as demolition work begins.

Many bazaars and garden fêtes have taken place in Snodland over the years, but the parish church fête of 19 July 1911 seems to have been more lavish than most. The local upper-class families attended this one in force.

The nearest tent in this view was manned by Mrs Roberts, wife of the cement works owner, and the next two by Mrs Gash and Mrs Freeland, wives of local doctors.

William Booth, founder of the Salvation Army, on a visit to Snodland on 22 July 1908. In those days there was no fear of causing traffic problems at the main crossroads! Note the balcony that once existed on the side of the Bull Hotel.

It is said that Dr John Palmer (1852-1914) was the first person in Snodland to own a motor car. Perhaps it was this one, pictured outside the surgery at the lower end of the High Street. Dr Palmer proudly sits behind the steering wheel, while his chauffeur, E. Ensal, is relegated to the passenger seat. By Christmas 1910 this D2439 had been exchanged for a later and larger car, the D4478 (of which a similar picture was taken).

Henri Salmet was one of the best known early flyers. He was forced to land at Paddlesworth on the return journey of his record flight from London to Paris in March 1912.

On one occasion Salmet asked a local lad to make sure he held the rear of the aeroplane high when preparing for take-off, but unfortunately the boy held it too high, so that the propeller gouged the ground and was broken. The airman's rest in the haystack was perhaps unintended.

Unveiling Ceremony, War Memorial, Snodland.

The war memorial in the cemetery was unveiled by Rear-Admiral Sir Doveton Sturdee (victor of the Battle of the Falklands in 1914). Earlier Sturdee had been presented with an address by the parish council, before joining the procession to the cemetery.

On 5 August 1944 Malling Road was hit by a flying-bomb, causing great damage and loss of life.
Below: The devastation in Malling Road seen from the north east.

Snodland's Salute the Soldier Week.

July 15th - 22nd. 1944.

Saturday, July 15th.

2.30 p.m. GRAND SERVICES and CARNIVAL PROCESSION. Starting Point New Road. Parade Marshal C/O Wooden Salute to be taken by Major Leigh at the Central School Grounds. Prizes to be presented by Mrs. Combe.

6 to 8 p.m. CHILDREN'S SPORTS at the Central School playing fields

7 p.m. GRAND DANCE at the Institute The Royal West Kent Dance Band. Admission 3/- Forces 1/-

Entries for Fancy Dress to be handed to Mrs. Rich, Queens Avenue, by July 12th.

Sunday, July 16th.

8 p.m. UNITED EVENING SERVICE in Cricket Meadow.

Monday, July 17th.

7.30 p.m. GRAND WHIST DRIVE at the Institute. Admission 1/-

Tuesday, July 18th.

3 p.m. OPEN AIR CINEMA SHOW on All Saints Rectory Lawn. Admission 6d.

7.30 p.m. N.F.S. CONCERT PARTY at the Devonshire Rooms. Admission Reserved 2/- Unreserved 1/6 and 1/-

Wednesday, July 19th.

7.15 p.m. SNODLAND CHORAL SOCIETY present "MERRIE ENGLAND" with Orchestral Accompaniment at the Central School Hall. Admission Reserved 2/- Unreserved 1/-,

Thursday, July 20th,

7 p.m. A.T.C. DISPLAY at the Central School.

7.15 p.m. SNODLAND DRAMATIC SOCIETY present "FAMILY AFFAIRS" at the Devonshire Rooms. Admission Res. 3/- and 2/6 Unres. 1/6.

Friday, July 21st.

7 p.m. COMIC FOOTBALL MATCH in Cricket Ground followed by a MOCK AUCTION.

Admission 1/- Children 6d. (If wet) Social and Mock Auction at Devonshire Rooms.

Saturday, July 22nd.

PENNY TRAIL by the Girl Guides.

2.30 p.m. CRICKET MATCH Shorts v Rootes Maidstone

2.30 p.m. BABY SHOW at Ivy Meath, (if wet) at Devonshire Rooms. Admission 3d.

6 p.m. BOWLS TOURNAMENT at Hook's Sports Ground. Admission 6d.

7.30 p.m. DANCE by the Home Guard at the Drill Hall.

Entries for Baby Show 3d. each,. to be handed in by July 19th. to Mrs. Stotesbury, Mobberley. Malling Road.
Miss Dale, Bramley Road. Miss Stone. Bramley Road.

The programme of fundraising events in 'Salute the Soldier Week', 1944.

The Observer Corps leads the United Church parade along Holborough Road on 13 May 1945.

Eight
Industry

Although headed 'Snodland Paper Mill, 1932', this postcard also shows some of the other industries formerly at the east end of the village. The gas works, the Lead Wool Company and buildings associated with Peters' cement works are on the river bank to the north of the parish church, while centre-left near the bottom of the picture is the paper bag factory.

A paper mill has been in continuous production in Snodland since at least the 1730s. Charles Townsend Hook and his father Samuel purchased the mill in 1854. This headed paper dates from the First World War (at which time the legend at the top was added). The inset is reproduced from a trade card of 1886.

Four emblems or logos of local cement manufacturers: Hilton had interests elsewhere, as well as at Hilton, Anderson, Brooks & Co., Manor Works, Halling (to around 1925); William and Henry Peters at Wouldham Hall (to around 1925) operated what was reputed to be the largest cement factory in the world; William Lee and Alfred Smith at Halling (to around 1931); Burham Brick, Lime and Cement Co. worked intermittently until 1941. These emblems would appear on company products such as barrels.

Paper and cement production were the keystones of Snodland's industry. In his development of the paper mill, Charles Townsend Hook (1832-1877), pictured here, together with William Lee at the cement works, led Snodland from its traditional agricultural life to one in which it became a significant centre for industry.

William Lee (1803-1881) acquired the lime works at Halling in 1846, creating chalk pits on the Snodland-Halling boundary. Here he is in 1878 with his daughter Anne Roberts (1823-1881), and her son William Henry Roberts (1848-1926), who became a partner in the business. His son William Lee Henry Roberts (1871-1928) founded his own business, the Holborough Cement Company, in 1923. This was acquired by APCM in 1931 and its assets are currently owned by Lafarge Cement UK.

On 12 August 1906 the paper mill was totally destroyed by fire (see chapter seven).

Rebuilding took two years and the mill reopened in 1908. The building shown here has itself recently been demolished because parts had become unstable.

Apart from a few pictures it is regrettable that all the early mill archives, having survived the great fire in 1906, were pulped some fifty years ago. This view dates from 1887.

A similar view of the paper mill in 1960.

The Hook family had tried operating a silk factory from 1866, but this failed. In 1883 James Nichols & Son purchased the site and set up their paper bag factory. This flourished until July 1981.

Another view of the paper bag factory from the south east.

This fuzzy picture shows James Nichols and his son proudly standing beside the Lock Seam machine which they invented and patented, and which allowed a new means of sealing the bags.

One of the machines used for printing the bags.

Lime works began operating at North Halling in 1799, and 100 years later were trading as Trechman, Weekes and Co. As this pre-1920 picture shows, the works were built at Whornes Place, the home of the Marsham family, Earls of Romney, who owned much of Snodland, Halling and Cuxton as well as much other land elsewhere from the seventeenth century until 1808.

The pit on the opposite side of the road was called Bores Hole, seen here in around 1920.

This picture comes from a postcard issued by the 'Additional Curates Society' of Westminster. Its caption reads: 'Halling was only a village thirty years ago. The cement workers and their families have brought the their number to over 2,000 at the present time. The A.C.S. helps to provide them with an additional clergyman so that the two parts of the parish, Upper and Lower Halling, may both be well cared-for.' Hilton and Anderson's cement works was built in 1878 to replace a lime works on the site.

The Pit & Hills, Halling.

A view of the pits serving Hilton and Anderson's works.

The most western part of Batchelor's (formerly Formby's) pit workings.

Workmen in Lee's pit, Halling, *c.* 1895. This photograph is on copper.

The Holborough cement works in 1930.

The Holborough cement works shortly before closure and demolition in 1984.

The gas works in Church Field, 1930.

The brick works at Ham Hill, 1930.

Nine

Schools

Snodland Central School staff, 1935. From left to right, back row: Messrs Jones, Rice, Lewis, McGahey, Bayliss, Rush, Hatton, Oliver. Middle row: Mrs Thomas, Miss Levy, Miss Cutbush, Mr E.W. Ray (headmaster), Miss Lusty, Miss Clow, Miss Barnett. Front: Miss Kimber.

The first school in Snodland was begun by the parish clerk, William Lewis, in 1762 in his own house in Brook Street. Lewis died in 1797, but in 1800 John May set up a charity to enable twenty poor children from Snodland and ten each from Halling and Birling to be taught there for free by a schoolmaster. In 1867 the old buildings were replaced by new ones, which were further enlarged in later years as the population expanded. These were the National Schools, in which Church of England teaching had a high priority. The building of the bypass required the school to be moved to Roberts Road, and the old buildings were closed in 1979. The picture shows them shortly before demolition.

The staff on 10 March 1879. From left to right, front row: Sarah Plowman, mistress of the girls' school, Tom Hilder, headmaster, Annie Morris Finch, mistress of the infant school (which had recently been separated from the girls). Behind are their pupil teachers: Kate Boorman, Edith Gammon, George Pring, William Gooding, Clara Masters, Fanny Field.

These two pictures were also taken on 10 March 1879. One is of the girls' school and staff, the other the boys' school and staff – Mr Tom Hilder, the headmaster sits on the right-hand side. Presumably there was a similar picture of the infants' school, but no copy has yet come to light.

Older pupils at Brook Street, 1947/48. From left to right, back row: G. Whitehead, D. Hudson, B. King, P. Green, A. Collison, S. Taylor, J. Harewood, A. Ashbee, T. Burtenshaw, B. Norris. Third row: B. Sunnucks, K. Ballard, J. Holmes, L. Taylor, D. Sage, K. Hearnden, A. Turnbull, Y. Latter, J. Holmes, R. Knott. Second row: M. Holder, L. Roots, S. Saul, P. Hood, B. Caller, M. Everhurst, D. Golding, E. Williams, C. Mason, R. Reynolds. Front row: C. Martin, A. Knell, A. Gammon, R. Lawrence, A. Everhurst, M. Beaney, P. Stickings, B. Skinner.

Maypole dancing was an annual feature at Brook Street School fête. This picture was taken in July 1955.

A group of pupils of mixed ages at the British Schools, 1887. The teacher is Mr Moore, who had a crippled arm.

A netball team at the British Schools, 1924. From left to right, back row: Olivia Perrin, Mary Edgeler, Ruby Adkins, Doreen Law. Middle row: Hilda Collison, Connie Smith, Dorothy Witherden. Front row: Betty Hodges, Louise Ball, Violet Beaney.

British Schools 1924/25. From left to right, back row: Mrs Leonard, G. Monk, E. Knott, G. Parris, E. Wilford, M. Hasemore, M. Johnson, E. Lambert [some missing]. Fifth row: B. Booth, G. Giles, W. Stevens, F. Bishop, V. Street, W. Eastwood. Fourth row: J. Tapp, C. Norley, E. Elliott, W. Jessup, E. Langridge, F. Cole. Third row: C. State, F. Taylor, Bridges, Collison, H. Barnes, N. Tubb. Second row: J. Botten, J. Chambers, E. Pearson, B. Russell, J. Langridge, E. French. Front row: W. Brooker, D. Jackson, W. King, F. Mantle.

Snodland Central School county representatives and relay team, 1932. From left to right, back row: Marjorie Fielder, Edna Lambert, Stanley Groves, William King, -?- , -?- , Evelyn Hunt. Front row: Joan Brighting, -?- , Howard Morrison, Cecil ?, ? Day.

94

Class 4A1 in 1951/52. From left to right, back row: M. Gardner, M. Austin, S. Sutton, M. Reynolds, J. Wilson, R. Last, P. Deer, J. Tomlin, V. Castle, H. Everhurst, R. Adams. Third row: R. Francis, R. Humphreys, R. Guntripp, J. Coomber, E. Wooding, B. Lamb, P. Murray, P. Buss, J. Hills, I. Blackman. Second row: M. West, P. Edwards, J. Banfield, D. Bates, D. Harewood, Miss Barrett, M. Chandler, H. Barnden, S. Edwards, B. Keeley, I. Hanchett. Front row: A. Earl, J. Broad, R. Coster, L. Bridger.

Dinner time in the hall at St Katherine's School, around 1950. The building is now part of Holmesdale Technology College.

A happy group of pupils at St Katherine's on the same day. To judge by the milk drinkers, it is break time.

Mr Thornhill began his private school in May Street in 1885, with one pupil. It quickly expanded, and in 1888 he and his wife moved to the newly-built Tudor House in Malling Road, where this now damaged picture was taken.

Ten
Recreation

The Women's Institute at their annual party, probably in 1954. From left to right, back row: -?-, -?-, Mrs Collins, -?-, E. Brown, V. Larkin, M. Stone, F. Stroud, -?-, -?-, -?-. Middle row: -?-, -?-, Mesdames Austin, Harrison, Rutt, Holmes, Capon, Rabjohn, -?-, Keating, -?-. Front row: -?-, Mesdames Morhen, Hansell, Barnes, Smith, Knell, Austin, Hayward, -?-, Wanstall, Cochran.

Snodland Bowls Club, 1927. From left to right, back row: Messrs Pay, -?-, Baldock, -?-, Piper, Hammond. Front row: -?-, Messrs Monk, Lavender, Butcher, Thorndycraft, Hinds.

Snodland Bowls Club, 1942. From left to right, back row: Messrs Reeves, Moore, King, Robinson, Piper, Hodgson, Stevens, Finch, Harris, Gates. Front row: Messrs Ashbee, Gower, Langridge, Mrs Hughes, Mrs Hodgson, Dr Coombe, Mrs Baldock, Mrs Bell, Mrs Jackson, Mr Large; Miss R. Hughes (in front).

Snodland Cricket Club, 1912. From left to right, back row: C. Skinner, ? Ponds, ? Randall. Middle row: E. Parks, ? Coles, A. Glover, E.H. Edgeler, -?-, ? Hawks. Front row: A. Baldwin, E. Chapman, ? Budden, Horace Pile (whose occupation was recorded as 'professional cricketer' in the 1901 census; he was aged fifty-three in 1912), A. Fowle, ? Fowle.

Snodland Community Cricket Club, 1956. From left to right, back row: R. Hill, C. Hale, D. Fielder, P. Hollman, A. Wenham, R. Hammond, M. Fielder (scorer). Front row: C. Harrington, C. Smitherman, J. Hammond, B. Fearn, D. Coomber.

Townsend Hook staff cricket, 1963.

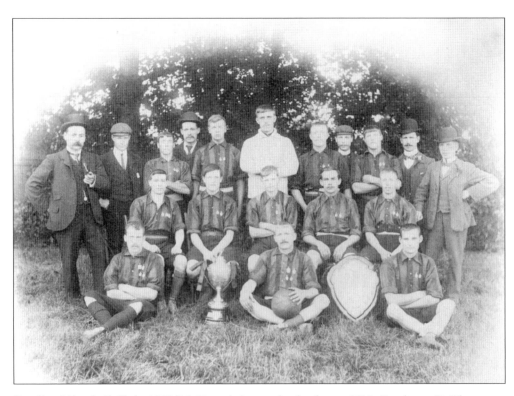

Snodland Football Club, 1903/04. From left to right, back row: W.J. Stephens, E. Chapman, J. Warrell, G. Peck, L. Harrington, I. Stevens, C. Knott, J. Knell, B. Atkins, H. Tremlett, T. Burke. Middle row: R. Wells, F. Peck, H. Preston, A. Izzard, C. Skinner. Front row: J. Wenham (vice-captain), H. Mayatt (captain), G. Chapman.

Snodland West End Football Club, Monk's Head, 1928/29. From left to right, back row: Messrs Bridger, Maytum, Beaney, Flint, Everest, Maytum, Allard, Hills, Sales, Kealey, Nye, Schooling, Eves. Middle row: Messrs Beaney, Burton, Norris, Everest, Flint, Stevens. Front row: Messrs Crabb, Palmer.

Townsend Hook Football Club, 1931/32.

The penny-farthing club outside
The Bull in the early 1880s.

E.H. Edgeler took part in many local
cycling events around 1900. Here he
shows off some of his trophies. Races
were held around the cricket field.

Snodland and District Choral Society was founded in 1929. This photograph was taken at their inaugural concert in 1930 with their conductor Mr C.F. Butcher in the front row, centre.

Ladies in Waiting was a ladies-only play presented by Snodland Drama Club in 1939, when men were likely to be called away on war duties. The cast are, from left to right: Laura Peck, Doris Walker, Lois Hambrook, Marjorie Stone, Joan Lucas, Eileen Taylor, Elise Revill, Florence Mathews, Monica Stedman.

Scout camp on Holly Hill, *c.* 1925. From left to right, back row: C. Hendy, A. Peck, S. Edmonds, -?- , M. Atkins. Middle row: -?- , F. Stone, L. Fuller, -?- , Mr Deuchars (headmaster at National School 1925-30). Front row: -?- , ? Cooper, T. McCoy, -?- .

Guides (Rangers) at their summer camp at Belmont Park, Faversham, in 1936.

Eleven
To Birling

The centre of Birling, before the Lych gate was added in 1897 as a memorial of Queen Victoria's Diamond Jubilee.

The demolition of Rookery Farm prior to the building of Rookery Farm Estate in 1962. It was a fine old Georgian house, but regrettably no other picture of it has come to light. The farm was quite extensive, stretching over what is now most of the southern part of Snodland.

In 1693 Snodland paid £4 10s to the parish of Birling for the right to include Grove Farm within Snodland parish. Although the farm was of great antiquity, the farmhouse had been rebuilt several times and ceased to operate in the 1950s. It was formerly sited to the left of this view, pictured here in around 1950.

Leg Lane Corner, Birling, around 1908. The former vicarage, now called Langold House, is out of view to the left.

Vicarage, or Langold, House, around 1860. It was enlarged soon after this picture was taken when Edward Veasey Bligh (briefly a curate at Snodland) became vicar of Birling in 1865. He had complained that the 'Lodge' in Snodland was 'a very tiny habitation', so perhaps this imposing house pleased him more.

An early rectory was once on the bank to the right of this view, pictured here in 1904, from which Parsons' Corner gets its name. The road to the left leads to the hamlet of Stangate and the Downs.

Stangate has changed very little over the years.

Birling Place, near the escarpment of the Downs, has been inhabited since at least the twelfth century. Its construction on a mound and with a defensive wall may indicate even earlier occupation.

Members of the Nevill family have lived at Birling Place since it was acquired through marriage in 1435.

William Nevill (1792-1868), fourth Earl of Abergavenny, was born at the family's Eridge estate and came to Birling as vicar in 1817. In the mid-1830s (exact details remain unknown) he built a large manor house some way to the north of the church. The photograph dates from about 1860 and shows the south-east side of Birling Manor.

Birling Manor, viewed from the south-west side.

The gatehouse to Birling Manor is situated to the north of the church.

On 17 January 1917 Birling Manor was completely destroyed by fire. This had started in the servants quarters, but the best efforts of several local fire brigades failed to contain it. Fortunately there was no loss of life and many of the valuables and furnishings were saved.

After the fire the Nevill family were forced to move to Birling House, built for William Henry Roberts in 1875. Roberts had moved to Holborough Court, Snodland, in 1886.

There are several photographs of this 'freak of nature', when the chestnut tree by the church bloomed twice in a year. Unfortunately this second bloom of October-November 1906 proved fatal, for the tree died shortly afterwards. The village forge can be seen in the background.

This view has hardly changed over the years. The school building on the right now serves as the village hall, and the forge on the left still operates.

Birling School pupils, 1905.

The Bull Inn, pictured around 1880 when Alfred Capon was landlord. Victuallers here have been traced back to 1647.

A 1930s view of Birling village centre.

Twelve

Halling

An early twentieth-century composite postcard showing views of both Lower and Upper Halling

The parish church of St John the Baptist, viewed from the east end. This engraving was prepared for Stockdale and issued in 1810.

Halling church before 1877, showing the original tower. This was rebuilt to its present state in 1892, when the clock was also added.

The post office (when Sarah Brigden was postmistress) and James William Dunford's grocery shop in the 1890s. Members of the West Kent Yeomanry are posing for the photographer.

Opposite the post office is Manor Farm House. The southern side with its fine door dates from the early nineteenth century, but the brick facing of the northern side may hide a much older building. This postcard is postmarked 1911.

The old Five Bells public house opposite the church, around 1908. Surviving manorial records show that this served as the court lodge for the Bishop's manor of Halling (which included Cuxton and large parts of Snodland).

The Institute shown in this view, postmarked 1904, has recently been replaced by a new building.

The junction to Upper Halling (left) and Strood (right), 1917. The forge house is just out of sight on the left-hand side. Very little of this scene remains today.

A 1930s view of Kent Road, with Edward Mutimer's grocery shop on the corner.

Vicarage road: the way to Upper Halling and the hills.

The High Street from the south, showing Poynder Terrace on the left and Hilton Terrace on the right, around 1920. The thatched building on the right is The Walnut Tree.

The Walnut Tree was an off-licence demolished in the mid-twentieth century.

Robert Ashby's wagonette is called into service here for the Five Bells Cork Club, complete with mandolin players.

The Mid Kent Water Company was formed in 1889 and within twenty years was serving eighty-five Kent parishes. The main works were in Halling and the offices were in Snodland. This postcard is postmarked 1915.

A view towards the north east with Court Farm, centre left, the Pilgrim's Way, sheltered by the trees, and Hilton & Anderson's Manor Works in the distance.

Portland Row is typical of the housing built by cement company managers like William Lee and Hilton & Anderson for their ever-increasing workforces.

The wayside chapel of St Laurence, Upper Halling, dates back to at least 1300. It was a casualty of Henry VIII's reforms and in its time has served as a wheelwright's shop and, currently, as houses.

The Street, Upper Halling is actually part of the so-called 'Pilgrim's Way'. This view appears to date from around 1940 or perhaps a little earlier.

New building at Upper Halling, also pictured around 1940. The Robin Hood public house is at the far end of the right-hand line of buildings.

Halling athletic sports, 1907. Messrs Hilton and Anderson, who no doubt employed many of the competitors, are seated in the middle of the second row. Next to them is the vicar (fourth from left) and his curate wears a straw hat in the front row.

Cycling was very popular in the area from the 1880s onwards. One mile, two mile and three mile races in particular were keenly supported.

Halling ladies cricket team playing RAF men billeted at Lee's pit, Warship Week, 1942. The ladies are, from left to right: Myrtle Tomkin, Maisie Bridges, Freda Comber, Mavis Tomkin, Dorothy Durling, -?- , Mary Wilkins, Pat Tomkin. In front are Len Heighs and Ted Hanchett.

An old view of Bourne House in Halling High Street, with adjacent shops.

Each year from the mid-nineteenth to the mid-twentieth century, the Royal Engineers practised bridge-building across the Medway between Wouldham and Halling. The postcard featuring this picture (from the Wouldham side) is postmarked 10 July 1914, just a month before the outbreak of the First World War.

The Bailey Bridge between Halling and Wouldham was erected during the Second World War, but was removed soon after.

Halling Ferry operated for 600 years, but finally closed in 1964.

The *Lee*, a steamboat built at Cowes for Lee's company, is seen here in 1890. It often took company members to see the barge races.